T0077951

WHEN FOUNDATION IS DESTROYED:
THE SOLUTION TO LIFE'S PROBLEMS

MERCY ZANG

BALBOA.PRESS
A DIVISION OF HAY HOUSE

Copyright © 2021 Mercy Zang.

All rights reserved. No part of this book may be used or reproduced by
any means, graphic, electronic, or mechanical, including photocopying,
recording, taping or by any information storage retrieval system
without the written permission of the author except in the case of
brief quotations embodied in critical articles and reviews.

Balboa Press books may be ordered through booksellers or by contacting:

Balboa Press
A Division of Hay House
1663 Liberty Drive
Bloomington, IN 47403
www.balboapress.com
844-682-1282

Because of the dynamic nature of the Internet, any web addresses or
links contained in this book may have changed since publication and
may no longer be valid. The views expressed in this work are solely those
of the author and do not necessarily reflect the views of the publisher,
and the publisher hereby disclaims any responsibility for them.

The author of this book does not dispense medical advice or prescribe the use
of any technique as a form of treatment for physical, emotional, or medical
problems without the advice of a physician, either directly or indirectly. The
intent of the author is only to offer information of a general nature to help
you in your quest for emotional and spiritual well-being. In the event you use
any of the information in this book for yourself, which is your constitutional
right, the author and the publisher assume no responsibility for your actions.

Any people depicted in stock imagery provided by Getty Images are
models, and such images are being used for illustrative purposes only.
Certain stock imagery © Getty Images.

Bible scriptures were taken from the KJV

Print information available on the last page.

ISBN: 978-1-9822-7034-6 (sc)
ISBN: 978-1-9822-7033-9 (e)

Balboa Press rev. date: 06/25/2021

CONTENTS

CHAPTER 1

What Foundation Means in This Context

The foundation is the most important part of anything we start and anything that we get involved with in our lives. It has many definitions. It can be referred to as the beginning of a process, the root of something new, the birth of something new, or the beginning of a new situation or circumstance. The foundation is whatever is done first in order to bring something into existence. It is the genesis of a new thing that can be referred to later on as the pillar of its perceived structure or the reason for its current strengths or weaknesses. Because foundation has to do with 'the beginning,' the foundation of anything we do is supposed to be treated carefully because it will determine the outcome of that situation in the end. For instance as Christians, when a person decides to start doing something without approval from God he or she is literally building on a weak foundation. The Bible speaks about foundation in many scriptures but the most popularly known verse is in the book of Psalms 11:3 which says, "If the foundation be destroyed what can the righteous do." This passage implies that our foundation can be a source of battle even for a righteous man. It is so crucial that even the innocent can be born a victim of turmoil, a man without any bad records can be accused of sin, and a Christian can be involved in great battles because of what the people in the past generation or family line did or are still doing.

This is why the foundation should always be handled with caution. Not many people know how important it is to get it right in the first place, but most of the problems we face in life today come from the root of our foundation or how we started ourselves. For instance, imagine when we want to build a house. We start by creating the foundation first, where the house will be raised from, and so if the foundation is not well structured it will only be a matter of time before the house will start having problems from the root, which can lead to a collapse in some cases. It doesn't matter how long it will take, if a house is not well structured, one day it will begin to shake or even collapse. On the other hand if a house is well structured it could last for many centuries and could be used and passed on from generation to generation without any disaster. The only thing that may let the house fall is if it is being demolished for another structure. This is simply how a foundation works in the life of a man.

In 1 Corinthians 3:10-15, Jesus Christ described a foundation using a house. This scripture describes the foundation of a man and how important it is to build a strong and solid foundation that cannot be moved in tough times. The foundation could determine how far a man can go in life as well as how long a man may live on earth and also how far he could go in making an impact in this world. Do not forget I said "could" because at the end of the day, God has the final say, but man has the duty of restructuring his foundation with the right attitude towards life in order to meet with God's agenda. The foundation of a man can bring limitations to one's life and it could also bring promotion and success depending on if it's a good or bad one. When a foundation is bringing forth good fruits it's either the foundation has been corrected or it has always been in a good standing with God, but when a foundation comes with lots of struggles, hardship or bad luck it means much has gone wrong over the centuries that needs to be corrected or one may not be in a good relationship with God.

If you feel you have been living your life the right way but nothing seems to be going well for you, before this book ends you will have a clear understanding of what the problem could be and how you can conquer it. So let me proceed with a good understanding from the word of God.

In the Bible, you can find stories of people who served God because of the choices of their fathers. You can also find stories of others who couldn't serve God because of the choices of their fathers too. Additionally, you can also find another set of people who didn't come from a background that serves God but still decided to serve God on their own. For example, you can read the story of Noah and how God picked him to survive the destruction that was to befall the people existing at that time. It was because of Noah that his wife and kids were saved also (read Gen 6-8).

Furthermore, in the Bible you could also find those who came from a good foundation and their fathers served God but they decided to turn away from serving God, therefore, creating another foundation for themselves. The Bible shows how God punished people for their unrepentant ways or wickedness. Truth is, God is not a beholder of iniquity and this is what made Him destroy almost everyone in Noah's time because of the terrible things they were doing. God never failed to bless those who did good by obeying His words. If we check out the story of Jonah who tried to escape from God's instruction for him to go to Tarshish we would see how God made him to be swallowed up by a whale as a punishment for rebellion. This just goes to show that wrong actions always have their repercussions all the time. The choices we make have a way of determining a lot of things and fortunately or unfortunately it could even determine the lives of those in our generation.

In many families today we can find repeated afflictions and patterns that happen to them. Actions that once happened before could repeat in the life of many others in the family lineage and it may only take the grace of God to stop these things from repeating themselves over and over again. It may take someone in the family who would do something different from others to be able to break the evil chains and repeated calamity in the family in order to bring about a change in the family. For example, if a man builds his life on stealing from others, he has already placed a curse on himself from God and also a curse from his victims. The kind of curse that these actions carry could appear in the life of his children and descendants yet unborn. When the victims that got robbed decide to place a curse on him it would either reflect on his life or on the life of his children. Sometimes the thief may never know why his life may be manifesting certain problems and may be thinking that it's just part of life, but the reality is, it's a curse. This is because there is power in the words of men. God has given man this power by His will and by the word of God (the Bible). Sad but true is the fact that those curses can manifest in the lives of the children of the thief who are innocent of the crime (read Proverbs 18:21 for more details). We must be careful of what we do today because what we do to others and how you make them feel can be a foundation of something good or bad. Negative words once spoken can determine a lot that will come to the man's life sooner or later. Curses don't die except they are addressed, and this is why we must take life seriously and be careful what we do.

Foundation and Your Ancestry

Ancestry can be referred to as one's family lineage, family background, generation or ethnic descendants. The foundation of every man begins from their ancestors. Our ancestors could play a major role in the life we come to meet in our early years on earth, especially if there's no one that is making a difference in the lineage by serving God genuinely and drawing many to God in that family. In many cases, whatever we experience from birth to age 9 is not always in our control because at that age we usually don't have an understanding of how to direct our lives to the right path with prayers. So the family lineage will influence our early years of life positively or negatively. The early family members' way of life and belief system could influence how the younger family members' life would go and also the kind of spirits that operate in the family. Fortunately and unfortunately, the works of our ancestors could determine the kind of good or bad things that happen in our lives because of the existence of family curses or blessings.

In the world today, many people are from a cursed background while others have some destructive covenants that exist in their family which would try to arrange the course of their lives or determine the outcome of their lives. For instance, if you come from a family where the ancestors were killers or rapists, this will cause certain kinds of curses to be in the family and some of these curses would be waiting to manifest in the life of people from such a family. The consequences of their actions could try to manifest from generation to generation. This is why we must all be careful with our actions so we do not become a source of problems to the generation that comes after us. We can find in some families today that there are particular things that keep happening to everyone as a pattern. These things don't just happen, because they have been happening from some point in the past and then the spirit of whatever problem it is keeps haunting everyone in the family because there is an unbroken curse or covenant. Do you know that our lineage could determine if we are dedicated to God or to the devil? Yes it could. It could also to a large extent determine how well our work with God can be, if we ever even were dedicated to Him. For example, if a family practices idolatrous worshipping and the people in that lineage dedicated everyone in the family to an idol, this could affect their lives because they would have strong covenants with false gods, and unless these covenants are broken such a person could have problems in their work with God and a lot of delayed or denied blessings that were originally ordained by God. Why is this so? It is because the idol powers would always be fighting them. If they have no idea of the dedication in their family then they would notice that there is great difficulty for them to connect with God as their Father. In such cases, one might not even be able to make heaven if you don't destroy the curses and covenants from the root because the powers are very manipulative. When there are curses and evil covenants in a family, it will continue to work against the life of the family members and try to control whatever happens to them if they allow it.

Not having proper knowledge about this would lead a man to live a life of regret and woe, and a life that is not originally theirs. They may begin to even blame others for their problems. The problems created by the ancestors could destroy a person completely if they are not addressed. This is crucial because if they never find out the truth, especially in time, it could lead to a wasted life, a destroyed life and may even cause premature death. But the truth is our ancestors have done their part and now it's left for us to do ours. It is never worth it to sit back and blame anyone for our problems. At the end of the day, our victory will depend on the actions we take to make a difference in the family.

Many people don't bother to find out about what happened in their ancestral lineage and they may never understand why their life is going the way it is going for them. They may just feel that things that are happening are the will of God and so there's nothing they can do about it. Careful evaluation is needed to destroy any rooted problems in the family. When I say rooted problems I mean the problems that have been there even before we were born. If a person doesn't understand their battles they will never win them. If a person's root is not examined and carefully dealt with, with the necessary prayers, some battles will follow us to the grave. I don't know how your life is going right now but even if it may look tough a change is possible, liberation is possible and even miracles are so possible with God (Matt 19:26). Many times we put the blame on other people for our issues, but the truth is those people could just be vessels used to fulfill a curse or a covenant existing in the family. So some of the bad things that friends or colleagues do to us are not really their doing but rather, there is a force behind it which could also be forces from our ancestors. Life is supernatural. Anyone who still looks at things from the natural state is living a lie. It is the supernatural that controls the natural things and if things are wrong in the supernatural it will affect what happens to you in the natural, and it will even affect who gets attracted to you in the natural. Strange but real, this is the reason a girl can be so beautiful but no one asks for her hand in marriage. The devil is the author of confusion and should take the blame for all that has happened to us right from the time of Adam and Eve, so don't waste any more time blaming others.

In many families today there are lots of challenges and some of these challenges happen collectively or to certain people. In some families the members always have common sicknesses happening to a number of them. Some of these sicknesses could be cancer, diabetes or high blood pressure and most of them are usually transferred from one generation to the other. Many people take these as normal and refer to them as inherited sicknesses. Some people feel that these sicknesses are just normal and natural and that they came from the blood by inheritance, but most of the time they are afflicted because of existing family curses that occur repeatedly to people in the same lineage. Our God is not an author of evil and does not wish for His children to perish. Many times these things repeat themselves because we are not aware that they are spirits and that they can be stopped. Definitely, there are family reoccurrences that are not the plan of God for our lives but because of iniquities that led to curses these things have been programmed to happen in some families. God is not to be blamed because He never planned for it to happen to us (Jeremiah 29:11). It's left for us as children of God to be aware that there are battles that we have to fight and win. When we ignore our battles we will never be able to live the life that we were destined to live here on earth.

Understanding the Term "Foundation" and How it Applies to Us

In the beginning of this book I described a foundation as a starting point. There's a saying that goes like this, 'The way you make your bed is the way you would lie on it.' It's so true because a person's circumstances are normally as a result of their own actions and this is simply how the foundation applies to us. And so this means that the manifestation of negative or positive experiences in our lives is from how we handle things and the actions we take. Truth is, despite what we face or see on a daily basis if we are not doing what is right then we are adding to our problems and not solving them. This is why we must never underestimate the power of doing the right thing at all times. For instance, if you decide to be a Good Samaritan to others and always be there to meet the needs of others, God would be moved to always make a way to help you because of your good deeds to others. This is why the Bible says whatever we sow we will reap (Gal 6:7).

When it comes to our foundation this means what you give out in your foundation is what eventually comes back in so many different ways. So just because you might have a bad foundation doesn't mean you should become bad too. It's better if we view our foundation as something that starts from us because it makes us see things differently and realize that our choices will make much difference. This will help bring a positive change in our lives because we would begin to think of how to change things. The truth is, before you even consider what someone did in your family or what happens in your family consider this, 'What have I been doing to improve the situation?' Are you making your generation better or bitter with your actions, habits, behaviors or influences? Are you living a life that has a positive impact on others? We must take the blame for what comes out of our life if we want to make a difference. We must stop blaming others and become world changers. We must live by what we believe or preach to others. It doesn't matter if you're different because a Christian is supposed to be different from others in a good way (Matt 5:16). Never sit down and blame your family lineage for what happens in your lives because you may never know the battles they had to fight alone to even stay alive and you never know if they never had anyone telling them the truth themselves. Always try to be a world changer and not a blamer. Creating your own foundation has to do with what you do, what you say, how you act, how you react. What we do in life has so much more power than we think, but many people have no idea. For instance, the Bible always talks about obeying the commandments of God because that will determine if you will make heaven or not, so when we build our foundation on obedience to the dictates and instructions of God you are preparing yourself to make heaven; it's that simple.

A Christian's foundation is so important because it can determine our work with God, it can limit our spiritual growth and even stop the beautiful plans of God for our lives or make one end up having a wasted and unfulfilled life which is definitely not God's agenda for Christians, so therefore a Christian is supposed to lay a good foundation for others to follow and not bother about what has been laid down for them before. The life of a Christian must be based on the word of God if you ever want to enjoy 100% of the benefits of being one. If a Christian doesn't lay a good foundation for themselves, their life becomes like that of an unbeliever and they will not be able to reach their highest potential in life. The life of a careless Christian is usually full of troubles. This is why the lives of many Christians are discouraging to unbelievers because unbelievers will be thinking that we Christians are not eating the fruit of our labor, or they may feel that we are serving God and still suffering. It's better to be an unbeliever than to be a Christian that frequently commits willful sin and is not living according to God's expectations. No Christian should live a wasted life. No Christian is meant to end up in hell fire. I pray and trust that you and I will inherit the blessings of heaven in Jesus' name. Let us be examples to the unbelievers so that they would want to know and worship our God, too.

Looking at life like our future begins from us is a positive way of thinking, and it really is the truth because we can create the outcome of our lives even if we never had a good start. We can still change our foundation by becoming the beginning of a positive change. When we go astray and live the wrong life this means we have decided to create or add to a bad foundation for ourselves and our descendants after us. What legacy are you leaving? Everyone on earth is here to make a marking, which marking are you making today for your family? We have to take our destinies in our own hands. Whatever consequences that our actions bring will become the outcome of our lives' issues and a good or bad start for those coming after us. If for instance you decide to become wicked and dreadful to others, especially people who are less privileged than you and you happen to have parents who are well known for being kind, peaceful and loving to others, then you are the destroyer of the foundation and the consequences of a destroyed foundation will come to you. This is why the Bible says that the Lord will visit the sins of the parents to the children even up to the third or the fourth generation (Deuteronomy 5:9). It is important to note that when God has an agenda for us we have to do things His way and not ours, or else He will be far away from us. If we do things our way when we have already been given directions from God then we are putting ourselves in the curse of rebellion and this could add to the problems in our foundation. The devil can come and do whatever he likes when we do things outside of God's will. Truth is, at the end we could be our own enemies and cause self-destruction to ourselves by giving the devil a foothold In our lives through disobedience to God.

Foundation and Your Bondage

Bondage could be defined as a state of being enslaved. So this means, anything that enslaves a person is their bondage and if someone is a slave to sin, then that sin is their bondage. Adam and Eve were the first to bring sin to the world by disobedience to God's instruction and thereby putting themselves in bondage of sin, which caused many changes in the world till today. People misinterpret what bondage really means. Bondage doesn't necessarily mean that one is trapped in a box or in some kind of imprisonment. Bondage could also be a stronghold. It could be something we can't do without or something that controls us beyond our abilities. It could also be something we adore even more than being in the presence of God. Most people who commit willful sin are in bondage even if they do not admit it because bondage could be a stronghold that can only be destroyed by divine intervention. Any sin we cannot stop easily is a bondage. If a person has anger problems they are in the bondage of sin and this is no different from the bondage of taking drugs. The most painful fact that sin itself is a bondage is why we must understand that until we learn the ways to overcome sin we would not be able to overcome bondage. For instance, with people addicted to drinking too much it means they will be prone to certain problems in their lives because the devil knows their weaknesses and therefore he would know how to control and manipulate them. The devil would always know how to get them to do what he wants because they have a sin that enslaves them. There is no way that individual could be free from the consequences of drinking or wasting money and even worse, destruction or death. This sin becomes a source of bondage in their lives.

Weaknesses are nothing to be ashamed of because everyone has weaknesses, but do you know that it is one hundred percent possible to get rid of your weaknesses? Most people think that weaknesses are supposed to be part of your life but no, as Christians we are to strive for perfection because we serve a perfect God. We should strive to be like our Father (Matt 5:48). We were brought here on earth for a purpose and we may not be able to fulfill it if we are comfortable with our weaknesses and feel that they are normal. Weaknesses come into our lives because of past events and experiences. They are never who we really are. Some of them are because of how we grew up, what we learnt while growing up and also when we let bad experiences change us negatively. Do you know that anyone can be transformed into someone totally different if they allow God to do that transformation through submission. Our weaknesses could be a source of serious problems if they are not removed from our lives.

Most times our culture, morals, rules and regulations, and ethics can be a source of bondage. For example, gay marriage is legal in some parts of the world and this is a total sin in the sight of God and so anyone into it is in bondage and the countries that allow them are helping to promote the bondage of sin in the world. When a man decides to marry a man or a woman a woman and they feel that there is absolutely nothing wrong with it they are already trapped. This is the kind of bondage that doesn't allow a person to know see the truth anymore. They are spiritually blind to the truth and they begin to change what is wrong to what is right and what is right to what is wrong. That is a very strong kind of bondage, unfortunately, and it calls for a deliverance because it consumes their sense of reasoning.

In another case, a bad foundation can cage a man's destiny. This means it can let our best potentials to be hidden or undiscovered. If we come from a foundation where people are not taught to love and care for one another, it affects the outcome of their decisions in life. Lack of good upbringing and godly ethics can make a man not reach his highest potentials in life, that is, if they decide not to work on themselves. A person can end up with caged potentials, caged talents, caged gifts and caged understanding because they are not used to living in the reality of the truth in Christ Jesus. This usually happens when a person was not given or taught the proper doctrines in life and have limited beliefs that hinder good results in certain vital areas in their lives. A caged mindset cannot do exploits because there are so many negative beliefs and sometimes these things are inherited. Yes, a man can inherit a bad perspective towards life from the blood of his parents. This is a spiritual thing and it's just like passing a bad attitude or a bad spirit to someone else. This is why we can find certain people today who don't believe in themselves and what they can achieve, and even when they are convinced it seems to be part of them and it will probably take a lot of working on themselves for them to change.

To overcome bondage we have to overcome our bad habits, beliefs, attitudes or wrong belief system and understandings and stick only to the truth which can only be found in the word of God (John 17:17). If we ever want to build a solid relationship with God we have to be able to overcome our weaknesses. Weaknesses will produce negative results no matter what we do. Whatever God has commanded us to do or not to do is possible and not hard, but this depends on our willingness to change and the level we want to get to in our walk with God. If we love Him we would do anything for Him. There's no weakness or sin that cannot be conquered, all we really need to do to overcome them is to pray the right prayers and have a genuine heart for repentance. If you are ready for a change, then start by praying this prayer often, "O Lord, give me the grace to overcome my weaknesses and glorify You in Jesus' name." You know what, as ordinary as that prayer looks, it is the kind of prayer that can change your life. I want you to know that because the supernatural things control the natural things in life we have the power to recreate ourselves. We can be whoever we want to be if we put our mind to it and pray about it. For those of you who don't believe in the power of prayers I want you to know that God is more interested in your repentance than your needs. He knows what you need and will never give you what will destroy you (James 4:2-3). To overcome bondage all we really need to do is cry out to God for mercy and destroy the yoke in the name of Jesus.

In the world today there are a lot of sayings and quotes which have a negative effect in our lives if we allow them. They could have a negative influence on our beliefs system. Some people use such sayings because they believe it's the truth. For instance believing that, "Whatever will be will be," is not the truth, but many people use this quote a lot. The quote has a way of shaping our belief system. I personally don't believe whatever will be will be, because, let's look at it this way for a minute. If whatever will be will be, then a lot of things that went wrong when they were not supposed to go wrong shouldn't have been. All the tragedy and unexpected happenings that occurred when the devil tries to steal, kill, and destroy (John 10:10), shouldn't have been because those were never part of the plan made by God. When a mother struggles and gives birth to a child and then after nine months the baby dies or dies at one month old, was that the purpose of having a child or rather was that meant to be? Of course not. There are so many incidents that have taken place that are unusual, unexpected and uncalled for. This is not God's agenda for your lives but the devil is out there trying to manipulate and destroy things. Adding to that, if a young lady struggles and graduates after her Bachelor's degree or Master's degree program and then suddenly, when it's just a few days for her to start a new job she dies, was that meant to be? Of course not, for we know that for those who love God all things work together for good, and for those called according to His purpose (Romans 8:28). Or what if a man dies all of a sudden on the day of his wedding ceremony, do you actually believe that was meant to be? There are certain things that happen and make us ask why. The word of God says that the plans He has for us are for good and not for evil, to give us a future and a hope (Jeremiah 29:11). God is not a destroyer of good things and His wish is to see us all doing well even as our soul prospers (3 John 2). He wants every one of us to have a great life while serving Him here on earth. All of these problems usually spring out because of wrong foundation that was created one way or the other. Remember I said, not praying before doing anything you want to do is creating a wrong foundation itself. I pray that as you take time to study this book you will learn how to fix your life the way God wants it to be.

We can also find slaves who love their chains. I got this statement from a book author, "Slaves who love their chains." It refers to people who love to remain in their bondage. To some people I have come across, the battles of life mean nothing to them, they take it like a normal part of life but that isn't true. Even when a sickness is happening to everyone in a family, it doesn't mean that it's meant to be especially if a Christian is among them. I have met a lot of sick people in my life who don't count their sickness or disability as a big deal because they feel it usually happens and anyone can be a victim so there's nothing more to it. It is like collecting a certificate for destruction when you see sickness as a normal thing that usually happens and is allowed to happen. It means one is accepting to be in the bondage of sickness and this is part of what is wrong with the world's belief system today. Read your Bible well and you will know that bad things don't happen without a reason. I don't care if the sickness is in the blood group or inherited from parents, but God didn't bring us here on earth to get sick and die but to live to a good old age with sound health. He brought you for a better purpose and things like sickness spring up to hinder the ability of a man and make him unable to fulfill his purpose effectively. Sickness is and will always be a limitation. There's no sickness God has not cured before. We just have to be in the right standing with Him and He will move mountains for our sake.

Some people are in bondage to fear. This could be an inherited behavior or from a bad belief system learnt over time. It can manifest as fear of human beings, fear of sickness, fear of what people think and even fear of death. The Bible says that God has not given us the spirit of fear but of power, love and sound mind (2 Timothy 1:7). Some people have not been able to achieve anything great in life because of fear. It has limited them and they are not able to do great things in their generation. The most sickly kind of fear we can notice today is the fear of what people will think. And it's very common. This type of fear can totally kill people's destiny. Fear is of the devil and in order for us to overcome it we must pray and then believe in the Word of God. As Christians we are supposed to be bothered about what God thinks us and not what men think. If you are one of those that prefers to please men rather than God or trust the words of men rather than the word of God, then you have signed up for a life of bondage that will lead to nowhere.

Foundation and Your Relationship with God

Our relationship with God is important and is the key to greatness in life. God knows His children and His children know Him (John 10:14). This means that some of us may even call ourselves active Christians and God may not even know them because of the kind of relationship they have with Him. The Bible describes this in these two chapters (Matt 7:21-23) and (John 10:27-30). If we call ourselves Children of God and we do not do the necessary things to build and nurture our relationship with God, we would not be in His inner circle even if we have been working with Him for 100 years. A man of God once said as I quote, "there are many people working for me as pastors that I don't know and I haven't even seen them before." This is the kind of relationship many people have with God. They know God but God doesn't know them because of their way of life.

It takes a lot to keep, nurture and grow a physical relationship, which is less important than the relationship we have with our Eternal God. One may even be very busy in the church, one may be a good Bible scholar, one may be loved by church members or even the most hard working in the church but when our actions are done with negative motives then we deceive ourselves because we are not really connected to Him. For instance, if the relationship that Mr. Sam has with God is based on what blessings he wants to get from God, then Mr. Sam is doing business and not really interested in pleasing God. This means Mr. Sam is only serving God for benefits and there is no strong connection and love for God. Be sensitive. If you were not aware of this before because no one told you the truth; well, now you know.

Foundation and Your Destiny

Our destiny has to do with our divine purpose. What then is divine purpose? This simply means the purpose and agenda of God for our lives before our existence on earth. That is to say, the blueprint of what we were made to do here on earth. Everyone has a divine assignment.

Some people refer to it as divine destiny. Everybody has one but we can still find a lot of people who think that life should be directed by ourselves. They feel whatever works for them is what they would go for or stick to. This is not true because the devil is a great manipulator and always working to take us out of God's will. I am sorry but anything cannot go when it comes to God, we are all here for an assignment. I pray that if you have not discovered your divine purpose here on earth, may the Lord open your eyes tonight to His revelation and agenda for your life in Jesus' name. Pray this short prayer before we continue. Say, "Oh, Lord, let Your will be done in my life and not mine, in Jesus' name."

Do you know that this simple prayer is very powerful because it means that you are ready to let your life go in the direction God wants it to go and not yours. This is the kind of prayer that heaven is always happy about. We must understand that coming to earth without fulfilling our destiny is a tragedy, we must take it upon ourselves to do the will of God or else we would be living a wasted life. A great man of God once said that the richest place on earth is the graveyard. Why do you think he said so? This is because a lot of people have come and gone without becoming the person God made them to be. They lived a stolen life. Some were supposed to be wealthy but never attained it. Some others were supposed to be great world changers but their foundation never permitted it. And unfortunately some were meant to be heaven-bound Christians but couldn't make it. To fulfill our divine purpose a lot of things have to be going well in our foundation. We have lots of people around us that God put there for a purpose. And there are people who will not be able to fulfill their destiny if we don't fulfill ours because they are divinely connected to us. This means we have all been given the grace to help others one way or the other. If a person is unable to fulfill their own destiny, it will affect some other people's destiny. This is why as Christians we all have to make up our minds not to be a hinderance to the purposes of God. We must choose if we want to live our lives for our selfish interests or for the interests of others? If you haven't started fulfilling your destiny then it's time to talk to God and get started. It's never too late when you are ready and when there is life and time ahead of you.

CHAPTER 2

The Foundation Relating to Man's Character and Its Consequences

Good and Bad Consequences of Foundation Relating to Man's Character

This section of the book describes a good and bad foundation from a different context so that we can better understand the attitude or behaviors of those who have a good foundation and those with a bad one. At the end of this chapter you will understand what it takes to live right or wrong and the result of it. In Luke 6:46-49, the Bible says that when a man hears the word of God and does it, he is like a man who laid his foundation on a solid rock and when the flood arose the house could not be shaken, but for the disobedient he is like one that builds his house on the earth and when the flood came the ruin of the house was great. When you read on you will more fully understand how a good foundation can lead to a victorious life and how a bad foundation can have the opposite effect.

The Good Foundation: A good foundation is one that is based on the word of God. It's a foundation that has been cleansed by the blood of Jesus Christ. It's based on truth and the perfect will of God. How does this type of foundation come about? It happens when there is an individual or a group of individuals in a family that have totally surrendered their lives to God and are out to do all it takes to maintain their salvation. It happens when there is liberation in a family and change has come into the lives of members of the family. If there were any bad things happening before in a family, a good foundation will stop them from reoccurring. It's a foundation based on the fear of God. A foundation where people are out to do good and to do the will of God no matter what it costs them. It's a foundation free from sorrow, tragedy, untimely death, failure, retrogression and many other bad experiences. A good foundation brings forth good fruits. It is filled with nothing but the joy of the Lord. There is no sickness and disease that can survive in a good foundation. The enemy finds no resting place on such a foundation and so he flees from anywhere the foundation is built on a solid rock. Here are some of the attributes of a good foundation:

Holiness and Righteousness: In a good foundation, holiness and righteousness is practiced as a way of life.

The love of God and humanity is very visible in the life of the individual with this type of foundation. The people here do not go out of their way to commit sin. They are out to set good examples in the sight of God and man. They hate to sin. Willful sin is a burden to their hearts. They depend on God and seek to do God's will at all times. They understand that the ways of the flesh only lead to destruction so they try to live their life according to the doctrines of the Bible. When there is holiness in a foundation, no power of curses and covenant can prosper there because there is no room to stay in their lives. Even if the devil was in charge before, the rules change automatically because this set of people are careful to do the things that are pleasing in God's sight. The Bible says that, when a man's ways please the Lord he makes his enemies at peace with him (Prov 16:7). Even if there are any problems from the past they cannot affect a foundation based on holiness and righteousness. God begins to fight for the people in this type of foundation. What was supposed to be a curse turns into a blessing. Psalm 1:1-3 says, "Blessed are those who walk not in the counsel of the wicked or stand in the ways of the sinners or sits in the seat of the mockers but delights in the Law of the Lord and they meditate upon it day and night. They shall be like a tree planted by the stream of waters which brings its fruits in its season, their leaves shall not wither and whatever they do they prosper." This means their lives are totally in line with the will and purpose of God and they do not believe in any other truth except the truth that comes from the word of God. The word of God is all they depend on in this type of foundation. Eventually no problem will come and overtake them because God gives them the power to conquer and win all their battles.

Love and Patience: Even the Bible says love is patient and kind (1 Corinthians 13:4a). A foundation based on love and patience is very powerful. If you read Romans 13:8 you will understand that love has no rules. It's the most powerful force for any type of success in life. When there is love and patience in a foundation, the devil leaves it in shame. People with this type of foundation love God deeply and are very patient with others. They fear God and appreciate God's love for themselves. They also appreciate people no matter who they are. They do not find it hard to do good to others. They try to live a life that is free from hate and bitterness. They are considerate and wish others well. They have nothing to do with wickedness. They show love to others when necessary without restrictions. The fear of the Lord dwells richly in their hearts and they live by what they believe in. This set of people knows that what goes around comes around so they try to show love often so that it can come back to them and their children. They hate to see the downfall of others. They do not like to see people in a bad or painful situation. They love to help others. They do not help others based on what they want or if they are in their family or not. They see all the people of this world as one family with God and therefore they do to others what they wish for themselves no matter who it is, not because they need something but just because they are genuine Children of God with loving hearts. Their ways pave the way for favors from God and man. God is so interested in those people who love others genuinely and patiently. (Romans 13:8). It would be difficult for the enemy to destroy the lives of those who constantly show love and patience to others, and no evil curse or family problem can stand where love is.

Selflessness and Brokenness: The people who build their foundation on selflessness and brokenness get their prayers answered so quickly. Things work out really well for them most of the time. Anything that doesn't work out for them is not the will of God. Psalm 51:17 says, "the sacrifice of God is a broken spirit, a broken and a contrite heart the Lord does not despise." Selflessness and brokenness has to do with forgetting about yourself most of the time and putting God first. It is having God's agenda and priority first place in your life. People with this type of foundation do not practice any form of willful sin. Willful can be defined as sin committed deliberately or with selfish propose. (Hebrews 10:26 talks about the consequences of willful sin). Selfless and broken people behave like they are dead to sin, anger, pride, jealousy and all the things people do and consider as normal nowadays. They have trained themselves with the help of the Holy Spirit to flee from selfishness, self-praise, self-love, self-glorification and almost everything that has to do with self-love. Self-love is considered as an attitude that displays inconsiderate, selfish and prideful behaviors. When we are selfless and broken we become vessels worthy to be used for exploits by God. He reveals His deep and secret things to such people (John 14:21). This set of people will be so anointed and considered as a great threat to the kingdom of darkness. These are the kind of people that are empowered to deliver others from their problems because God has empowered them to do so. God invests so much in them because they are not bothered about what they want from God but by what they can do for God. Their lives are full of testimonies because the devil cannot curse who God has blessed (Numbers 23:8). They are very quick to repent when they fall into sin. They remain humble and never tend to be self-righteous or better than anyone. They are cautious and careful to do the will of God and because of that, everything falls in place for them according to the will of God. In their hearts, sin is like a burden and they cannot afford to dwell in it. These kind of people can hardly fall for the devil's schemes because of their solid foundation in Christ. Whatever is meant to harm they will eventually use as a steppingstone for bigger breakthroughs in their lives. They are truly blessed folks.

Fear of God and Prudence: Those who build their foundation on the fear of God and prudence are wise indeed. The book of Proverbs speaks a lot about the prudent man as a wiser man than a simple man and also the book of Proverbs 9:10 says that the fear of God is the beginning of wisdom. This type of foundation is for those who are careful to do what is right in the sight of God, they are careful to obey the word of God, careful about how they treat people, careful about how they react to things, careful about how they serve God, and careful about how they live their lives generally. They don't just do things based on their feelings. Our feelings and flesh work together and remember the Bible says that the flesh profits nothing (John 6:63). Most sins that are committed are committed to fulfill the desires of the flesh, for instance, anger. Why people get angry is because their flesh has an ego that they must protect. Anger is not a character of the Spirit and in order to be a genuine child of God we must try not to give our flesh the attention it wants (Gal 5: 22-23). Some of these desires are lust, jealousy, pride, boasting, and greed. These are done out of self-love and self-will. People with fear of God and prudence know that they cannot be perfect but they try the best they can to do what is right in the sight of God and then keep away from troubles. They don't feel self-righteous and they are always humble enough to admit it and make their way straight with God fast when they are in the wrong. The mercy of God always speaks in their life because they are aware of what they have to do to maintain a cordial relationship with God. They are not careless. God promised to show mercy to the merciful in His word (Psalm 18:25). The people with fear of God and prudence receive mercy from God always because they know exactly what to do to get it, for it is by the mercy of God that we are not consumed (Lamentations 3:22). They don't have to be bothered about bad things happening to them because God is pleased with them (Proverbs 16:7). The bad situations in a family lineage will not affect them and because they fear the Lord, God will be fighting all their battles for them without resistance.

Blameless and Sincere: To be blameless and sincere in this context means doing all it takes in your power not to offend God or man. This is so achievable even if no one is perfect. People who build their foundation on being blameless and sincere sleep well at night. Have you ever heard the saying, "there's no pillow so soft as a clear conscience." This set of people are the kind of people that God loves to use for His work. They do everything possible to keep a good name and not to cheat others. I once had a friend who wasn't really a Christian but he just believed that what worked for him was never to repay people evil for evil. He said he had substantial evidence in his life of how God had been fighting for him when he had overlooked people's wrongs and allowed them to get away with their bad actions. At the end of the day things will end up working for his favor. He also said that he noticed that he ended up doing better than those who wronged him when it comes to success. With this kind of attitude God is ready to fight for you even when you don't know Him. People with this foundation receive the mercy of God in abundance. They are a blessing to the unloved. Even if they might have problems with their lineage, God will always be ready to fight for them if they come to Him. They have the kind of heart that can easily work with God so their prayers will be answered more quickly. They are not usually defiled because they keep away from all appearances of sin in order to live right. Even if they might have some bad habits, when they decide to give their all to God nothing can hinder their breakthrough. They are easily used by God to help others so they can never lack help, and God will also make a way for them out of their troubles. They are never defeated by foundational battles because God helps them out and their attitude paves the way for swift victory in their lives.

Forgiving and Unchanging: Those who have the attitude of forgiving others without changing their love for them are a very powerful set of people. This is a virtue of Jesus Christ and the most powerful virtue indeed that can help a man to come out of any form of bondage. The devil must have a foothold before he creates a stronghold, so the devil has no advantage over them because their heart is free from revenge. For if we forgive others their trespasses, our Heavenly Father will also forgive us (Matt: 6-14). The truth is, for most people in the world who lack faith it is because of the unforgiving nature in them. If a man lacks the ability to forgive others he will not be able to have the faith that God can forgive him. This is the simple truth. The state of one's heart when it comes to forgiving others determines the level of faith they can ever have. We must try to pray to God to take away anything in us that can hinder His blessings from coming to us. Forgiveness is the nature of love and a very powerful force for breakthrough. Are you holding anything against anyone? If yes, then drop this book and make amends immediately and see what a difference it will make in your life. Matt 6:14 makes it clear that when we are forgiving our prayers are answered. So then, people with this kind of foundation never get into problems that seem impossible to solve because God always favors them because of their kind heart. Because they show mercy they receive the mercy of God, and He also gives them victory. The Bible says that to the merciful, mercy will be shown (Psalm 18:25). So when we sow mercy, we will reap mercy.

Care and Compassion: Those who care about and have compassion for others are very useful in the world today because without them a lot of people would not have succeeded and some people would never have been happy or healed from a drastic situation. This type of virtue is important to man and God. Any Christian who does not possess care and compassion is not qualified to be one. These type of people are good listeners. They feel empathy for people who are in pain. They are a voice for the voiceless. They don't find it hard to volunteer to help the less privileged. They keep the secret of others and make people trust them no matter who it is. They are good givers. They have a kind heart and God blesses them with diverse creative ways to love and serve others. When an individual becomes very helpful and useful to God in the lives of others it is usually because that person is full of compassion and care for others. Galatians 6:2 says bear one another's burden in order to fulfill the law of Christ. There are many scriptures that show the importance of care and compassion, like Romans 12:15 that tells us to rejoice when others rejoice and weep when others weep. These kind of people don't go through problems that are overbearing because even the prayers of others are working for them. Their usefulness to the kingdom and to mankind paves way for their own victory in their own personal battles. God fights for them while they take care of the needs of others.

Prayer and Fasting: A person that prays and fasts is very powerful too. Although if a man has so much sin and doesn't ask God for forgiveness it could hinder his prayers from being answered. This set of people's efforts are never wasted because these are powerful tools for all Christians. Their persistent prayer and fasting brings breakthrough for them. No matter how bad a person can be, if they are consistent in prayer and fasting God will start to talk to them by dreams and revelations and they will know if their prayers are hindered or why they are hindered. This can help them change their ways to the one that pleases God. Prayer and fasting is the key to any form of deliverance. What a lot of people do not know is that we are permitted to talk to God about anything and everything. Prayer can change a man's ways and behaviors. It brings direction to a man's life. It helps to reveal the root of a man's problem and reveals how to fix it. With continuous prayers and fasting God by His mercy will come to rescue them from their problems. One great thing about this kind of foundation is that it is the best for spiritual growth. When you go further in this book, you will discover the essence of spiritual growth and power through prayer and fasting. It's definitely one vital key to freedom from any foundational problem in a family lineage.

The Bad Foundation: A bad foundation is the devil's playground. It's a foundation that is based on sin and the desires of the flesh. There is no genuine relationship with God in this type of foundation. It is based on satisfying self and its lustful desires. It's a foundation governed by the devil to bring destruction to mankind. The problems of life really started from a bad foundation. Like I said before, anything that is done outside the will of God is already a bad foundation no matter how right it may look. Generational problems are created from bad foundations and things will get worse over time if a change is not made. Once it is damaged from the beginning it will take a lot of effort to fix it. Most of the time I have noticed that people with this kind of foundation don't like to fix anything and they take all of life's challenges as if they were just meant to be. Once a foundation is good it never gets better, it only gets worse except by conscious and constant effort to please God in all ways.

Pride and Anger: When pride comes then comes disgrace but with the humble is wisdom (Proverbs 11:2). For the anger of a man does not produce the righteousness of God (James 1:20). Be angry and do not sin, do not let the sun go down on your anger (Ephesians 4:26). These passages and many others show Bible truth about those who build their foundation on pride and anger. This set of people are in bondage without even knowing it most of the time. Such an attitude towards life always brings shame, foolish decisions and regrets. A man of God once said that there are 23 types of poverty. Poverty is not only when you don't have money. But there is something called poverty of character, and anger and pride are one of them. Without a godly character (free from pride and anger) we would never be able to conquer and win the battles of life because the devil would have control over our minds. The devil would be able to steal blessings, breakthroughs, relationships, joy and favor from us. Pride is a killer and the devil was the first proud person on earth. Proud people are rarely used by God. Nothing good can be achieved with pride because it's the character of the devil. Don't get me wrong about anger, because anger can be handled with maturity and wisdom. We have to learn ways to conquer anger and not let it conquer us. To win foundational battles you must not be a slave to anger and pride.

Jealousy and Envy: Wherever there is jealousy and envy witchcraft is always in control. Many times people with this kind of foundation do unimaginable things that only add more problems into their generation. Jealousy is something that can be managed with wisdom. Wisdom is a principal thing but above all get understanding (Proverbs 4:7). People with this type of foundation use their weaknesses wrongly and it leads to suffering. They desire the wrong things, they do not put God first but have other things upon which they can waste their whole life doing. It's like having an idol, because having an idol doesn't really mean you're not serving God, but it is when other things are more important to us and then we lose focus on God. When people start to do anything to get what they want they create problems for their foundation by sowing bad seeds to get their pleasure. Being in the will of God is our decision and the only way to win the battles in life. Romans 12:2 says, "be not conformed to this world but be transformed by the renewing of your mind that we may prove what is the good and acceptable and perfect will of God." The attitude of jealousy and envy only leads to bad choices that can affect people and others in their family lineage because of the curses that can come from bad choices. For instance, if a jealous person decides to tarnish someone else's image or reputation because they don't want them to receive favor or promotion, it will only end up blocking their own blessings. God has called us to help others and not bring them down (Philippians 2:4). If we cannot help others, then we must never be a stumbling block to their progress. If we claim to be children of God, then jealousy and envy must be far from us in order for us to reap the benefits of being God's children and be able to break any generational curses affecting our lineage without hindrances.

Unforgiveness and Bitterness: Unforgiveness is one of the most powerful forces that blocks the Holy Spirit's entry into the life of a believer. It hinders faith from working and that's why you may notice many people who cannot exercise their faith (Read Mark 11: 22-26). It is like a poison that pollutes the spirit of man and makes it filthy in the sight of God. I remember in my younger days I used to keep malice and whenever I decided to make amends with the person it would be like a heavy weight had been lifted off of me, but then I would begin to get upset over the fact that I had actually allowed someone to burden my heart. Unforgiveness is really that bad. It is like a spiritual load that blocks one's progress and can cause serious health issues too. Some studies show that unforgiveness can cause cancer, depression, and other illnesses. This means unforgiveness can actually steal a lot from us. An unforgiving heart is a landing space for the devil and his demons to manipulate. It's also a major cause of delayed answers to prayers. It generally exposes one to internal and external torture. Most of the evil done to people on earth is because of unforgiveness. An unforgiving person will do dubious things and get cursed for it and this can become a generational curse if possible. It's also a major reason people will be going to hell because if we cannot forgive others how do we expect our Heavenly Father to forgive us (Matt 6:14).

Lust and Immorality: Some of the most dangerous problems in life can come into a man's life through lust and immorality. When a man is defiled it blocks answers to prayer and creates a ladder for the enemy to come into their lives and manipulate them. These type of people are frequent candidates for satanic manipulation. People who build their lives with this foundation have a whole lot of troubles to deal with. Immorality is sin against the body and this drives away the presence of God in a man. When the Holy Spirit is not functional in the life of a Christian, it is dangerous. 1 Corinthians 6:18 says that we should flee from sexual immorality because every other sin is outside the body, but this one is against the body. When people are deep in lust and immorality they start to make excuses for their sin saying things like, "it's normal," "I am human," "everyone does it," or "I am not fake like all these other pretenders." For these kind of people, problems will hit them so hard because the devil has his materials inside of them. They have sold themselves to the devil but may not know it. An anonymous person said that it's easier to deliver a witch than a fornicator. This is true because most of them doing this practice are deep into it and don't want to change except by divine intervention by the grace of God. They remain in their sins and the devil makes them form evil covenants with all sorts of demons and so they start to have physical problems that they cannot explain like sickness, disease, poverty and others. The consequences of the magnitude of their sin is then passed on to their innocent descendants when they refuse to change. This is because God would depart from them so they begin to suffer the consequences of their sin. The most painful thing about lust and immorality is the covenant they form with all sorts of spirits and then they pass it on to their children by heritage. And so the poor children begin to fight the same battles they fought without even knowing why just because their parents were far from God. I pray for God to deliver those in this situation by His mercies.

Selfishness and Greed: Selfishness and greed is a major cause of sin which may sometimes appear to be normal because some people were trained with this behavior. These type of people are self-centered and are all about themselves and their own well-being. They will do whatever it takes to meet their own selfish needs. They don't care about the well-being of others except if it is beneficial to them. They do not make friends for the sake of love because they love themselves 100%. They don't even care about following God's will in anything they do because they are not even patient enough to bear any suffering for a while. They blame others quickly and feel they are better off than others. God doesn't like selfish and greedy people because they are usually ungrateful.

They can never be satisfied with what they have and so greed is what can get them into destructive problems. Most of the problems they ever face are due to indiscipline and selfish interest. Psalm 10:3 says the wicked man boasts of the desires of his soul, and the one greedy for gain curses and renounces the Lord. This means greedy and selfish people are grieving the Lord every day. These type of people find it hard to get anything from God because they don't appreciate the things already done for them. They are never grateful for little things, so they find it hard to get more. This is the reason for James 4:3, which says that some people ask and do not receive because they ask to spend it on their passion. The problem of unanswered prayers and curses due to their lifestyle can affect generations to come.

The Consequences of a Good or Bad Foundation

There's a popular passage in the Bible that reads, 'the fear of the Lord is the beginning of wisdom' (Proverb9:10). This simply means that the only true wisdom there is, is the one that can be found in fearing God and living a life purposely to please Him and only Him. The people that have a good foundation are God fearing and so the presence of God is always with them. They put God first in every situation and make sure that they do not do anything without the approval of God and so whatever it is they lay their hands to do prospers. A good foundation is based on the word of God. Their lifestyle is based on the scriptural doctrines (Matt 6:33. Seek ye first the kingdom of God and its righteousness and all other things will be added to you) and so they do not find it hard to receive anything from God. The reason it may be hard nowadays to find this type of foundation is because there are a lot of people that came from a bad one and they are not ready to fix it, and for some of them who came from a good foundation they may not be able to maintain it if they live carelessly. Because a good foundation is a foundation that is God focused and purpose driven, they don't live their lives just any way that may randomly happen. They live a life of purpose and the first and most important thing they do is to form a covenant with God. Forming a covenant with God is by accepting Him as personal Lord and Savior and then living their life according to His doctrines so that you can get the benefits of true obedience according to the word of God (Read Psalm 1:1-3). People who have a good foundation don't just have the Holy Spirit in them but they also carefully adhere to what He says to them and this brings about positive results and unhindered blessings into their lives. When others have a casting down they would have a lifting up just because they follow the right teachings. They pay attention to how they live their lives, what they do, what they wear, how they talk to people and what is expected of them by the leading of the Holy Spirit. Even when there is a problem from the foundation they escape the consequences because they don't do anything to break their covenant and loyalty to God. The children that come from this foundation enjoy uncommon grace and mercy and they don't have to suffer for what their parents or ancestors did. Their lives can be referenced for good examples because it would always look as if they are perfect. They radiate in the glory of God forever and not for a short time. Although no one has a perfect life, this set of people are content with what God has provided them and they are grateful. They do not attach much importance to earthly possession but rather they focus on glorifying their Father in heaven. The Bible says a lot about God and His covenant and through it we understand that God is a covenant keeping God (2 Chronicles 6:19). To those who are faithful, God will be faithful to them because He is a God that follows His own principles (Exodus 19:5). You can read Joshua 23:14-16 to understand how God follows His own principles in dealing with man. So the reason those with a good foundation will always have everything working out for them is that this foundation is sustained by the fear of God and love for God.

So, these are the consequences of a bad foundation, a bad foundation is a destroyed foundation that can only be changed by divine intervention. It's simply the opposite of a good foundation. This set of people are either serving another god or have no god at all as they may claim, or it may be people that are calling themselves Children of God but don't have a covenant with Him. I can assume you might be thinking, "Well no one is perfect." True, but our God searches the intent of the heart and not really the sin itself and there's a big difference from committing sin intentionally and committing sin unconsciously or unexpectedly. This set of people have no fear of God. And so the punishment attached to disobedience always creeps into their lives.... Joshua 23:16 simply tells what the consequences of breaking the rules with God are and we must never be deceived because God cannot be mocked and whatsoever man sows he reaps (Gal 6:7-8). Most times these people don't have any covenant with God or they may have destroyed it, but they have it with the devil because there is no middle man when it comes to covenants, either you're in or out and the devil forms a covenant with people consciously or unconsciously whether they are aware of it or not if they do not establish and keep their covenant with God. And their lives would end up going in the devil's direction. It's a terrible thing indeed but what is even more terrible is that they would not be able to fulfill their purpose on earth except by divine intervention and if liberation takes place. A bad foundation is where bondage exists because one is living a life that is not based on God's principles so it would definitely not attract God's miracles and wonders.

There are many passages in the Bible that help us to know the significance and beauty of being a child of God. For instance the Bible says that the blessings of God make a man rich and add no sorrow to it (Prov 10:22), so how come we find a lot of rich people with problems like sicknesses, insomnia, and diseases? It's simply because their so-called achievement was gotten in a bad foundation and so it becomes attached to problems and sorrow. Let's face it, if we are not fully in Christ and we do not adhere to His words why should we now complain when things go wrong. Some people will do anything to make money. They will even kill to make money and they believe that when they kill to make money their lives are supposed to be rosy, but that is not possible. There are no two ways about it, we will reap what we sow and if we did not sow anything bad, but bad things are happening then that could be the fault of our parents, grandparents, or ancestors. One thing I know is that for those who are sincere to God, God will be sincere to them too, but when we are all about ourselves then God lets us face these foundation issues single handedly.

CHAPTER 3

The Foundation and our Dream Life

Although the foundation we come from could influence the kind of life we live today, it can also play a major role in our dream life. Dreams are windows that show pictures that can determine reality if not addressed. You cannot have a bad dream and just believe that it can never happen to you or someone you know or believe that it's just a dream. That is totally untrue, there is nothing like just a dream, dreams are so real. But many do not have the gift of discernment to interpret their dreams. If you are reading this book and you are a Christian and you can't interpret your dreams you are probably not having a good relationship with the Holy Ghost. You've got to take advantage of the Holy Spirit in you by nurturing the relationship. The Holy Spirit is our great interpreter (John 14:26). In the country I was born somewhere in Africa there was a lot of limited beliefs about dreams during my younger days. There was a belief that those who can interpret their dreams or those who see things before they happen are possessed by evil spirits. This is not true because the Holy Spirit is supposed to be our interpreter once we allow Him to take His rightful place in our lives (read 1 Corinthians 2:13). On the contrary, if someone can dream and the exact thing happens in reality, it's a good sign because it means the person could be a helper because they can let you know about any bad situation about to happen in time so you can pray against it on time. I've met a couple of people who have told me they don't dream or they don't remember their dreams. This isn't good either because they have no idea the direction their life's are going and they probably will be on the wrong path of life. Life is spiritual and it's the spiritual that controls the outcome of the physical. In this chapter I am going to let you understand why your foundation can determine the outcome of your dream life. In order to understand my teaching I would like to let you know that oftentimes, some people will say, "I dreamt I am in my workplace," "I dreamt that I was hungry," "I just dreamt about the place I am going tomorrow," "I just dreamt about that person I admire so much," etc. These are regular dreams that have to do with your thinking patterns so don't get me wrong, your thinking patterns count in our dream life to an extent. But what is more important or vital to note, are those regular or repeated dreams we have and we don't understand, or the ones we forget, or the ones that come as a revelation, or the ones that make you wake up with feelings that could be positive or negative.

Your Dream and Your Thinking Patterns: Ever wondered why the Bible says that as a man thinketh so is he (Proverbs 23:7). This is because what occupies a man's mind can influence his dream life and reality. Your thinking patterns affect your belief system and create imaginations that can manifest as dreams. Some ignorant people think that dreams are not real. I say ignorant because they have no idea that what they often think about could be used to manipulate their dreams. Although some dreams may appear to be just dreams or maybe because of a thinking pattern, we must carefully examine our dreams because there are a lot of things going on in our dreams that would help us know about the problems we are facing in our physical life. So if you are one of those who don't remember dreams you need to pray to God to remove all obstacles to your spiritual monitor (spiritual eyes). Let me give an example, if you often dream that you are driving to the office in your car but you forget to pay attention to the dream enough to see something different about you in that dream, then you would miss the problem that needs to be addressed. Let's say you are going to the office but you are wearing no clothes. But you did not pay attention to that part of the dream because you don't understand what it meant, but you understand that you are going to the office and that is good, then don't be surprised when a shameful problem happens to you in the office. Being naked in the dream in reality means expected shame and disgrace in real life. A lot of people don't know this because they don't just know or they are not discerning of it.

Therefore, not knowing how to interpret dreams would lead to manifestation of problems that would make one wonder why it might be happening to them. So pray this prayer if you can't remember your dreams. Say, "My Father, clear away every obstacle to my spiritual monitor by the power in the blood of Jesus." Or another way is when you wake up you can say, "Lord, every dream I have had that I cannot remember please reveal it to me, and anything that happened in the dream that is dangerous to me let the blood of Jesus cancel it in Jesus' name." These kinds of prayers are very helpful for those who are true Christians, so please make sure you are one.

Your Dream and Your Attitude: Sometimes when we dream and see ourselves doing things that we do not physically feel like doing or we didn't think about. It could be two things. It could be because these things are in us as an attitude and God wants us to know those things because He wants us to change something about ourselves, or it could be the attitude that the powers in our foundation want to bring into reality in our lives so that you can act as one of them and empower a curse to manifest in your life. When I say 'powers in the foundation' what I mean is that there are powers that know everything about us and our lineage and they try to force things into our lives from our dreams. When you're a weak Christian and not good in prayers these powers will mess your life up so badly just because you are far too weak to fight. Ever heard that Christians go through as many problems as sinners? Well, here are some of the reasons why. There are supernatural powers that exist and are bent on reinforcing the same things that happen in a family to make it happen over and over again to generations. So having a weak spiritual life with God can lead to a life that is as if it's under demonic remote control. You would see yourself doing things you don't want to do and getting results you do not expect to get in reality. This is to let you know that your attitude towards life can affect your dream life.

On the contrary, if you are close to God and you have been praying to Him about something, you might have such dreams so you would know why your prayers are not being answered and what to do about it. Sometimes God wants you to know that the things you are doing or that which you may be capable of doing and you don't know about, can hinder your work and growth with Him or can hinder prayers from being answered. To be able to discern your dreams you must be in a good and constant relationship with God and then the Holy Spirit will help you to interpret your dreams. Remember, there is no good thing that the Lord withholds from them who walk uprightly (Psalm 84:11). So if you know you have to change your ways you can pray this short and powerful prayer with faith: "Father, please help me to have the kind of attitude that attracts Your attention, in the name of Jesus."

Your Dreams and Your Beliefs: Sometimes it is what we believe in that manifests as dreams and then later affects our physical life. For instance, when someone has great fear of the unknown, your dreams will be a playground for the devil and this is why some people find it difficult to sleep alone or stay in a house alone and then this problem later affects their physical health. When you have great fear of the unknown there's no way you can avoid sickness in your body because you have already believed in the devil instead of taking authority as a Christian and praying to cancel it. The devil can manipulate any kind of sickness in your body and you will be too ignorant and scared to fight back in prayers. On the contrary, when you have a good belief of God and how great He is, it will also affect your dream life positively because the Bible declares that even the faith of a mustard seed can move mountains (Psalm 84:11b). So what we believe can manifest in dreams and bring either problems or great deliverance and victory to our lives. The tool of fear can really be a manipulation in one's dream life. This is why Christians should be good Bible readers, filling their hearts with God's words every day. But, warning: faith without works is dead. If you have so much faith and know the Bible but your life is not meeting up to the expectation of God, then your faith cannot produce anything. We have to be on good terms with God in order to have a faith that can move mountains. It's natural to fall out of faith when you are not intimate with the Spirit that produces faith in a man.

Your Dreams and Your Conscience: The good or bad we do in the sight of God will affect our dreams too. If you are living in sin then your dreams can be manipulated and blocked from your understanding or memory. This happens to people that are not in a proper relationship with God and don't have interest in the things of God. This is because you cannot regularly and constantly feed your flesh and expect to be active in the spirit. God will never force us to live right, we have to make that decision ourselves or else we would face the consequences (James 4:8). Remember the devil is out there looking for how to steal, kill and destroy (John 10:10). For those who are sinful, these kinds of people can even be killed by the devil through their dreams if they are not careful. They are not under God's protection because they are not known by Him (Matthew 12:50). But then again when we build a good relationship with God by adhering to His word, going to Church often, being productive in kingdom advancement, being good examples and repenting quickly from sin, then we can rest assured that our dream life will reflect our obedience to God and we will begin to know deep and secret things that will help us have a fulfilled life. This brings out dominion in one's spiritual life and gives one a life free from tragedy (Psalm 25:14). So, if you're still not born again then you have to pray to God and surrender your life to Him before it's too late. Do not waste your life outside the purpose of God.

Your Dreams and Your Foundation: The foundation comes from our family and its lineage so therefore it can affect our dreams depending on what the other people, our ancestors, or parents did. In order for us to understand better I would like to discuss the different kinds of dreams that can happen to a man with a bad foundation. When the foundation is destroyed, what can the righteous do?... The answer is nothing else but prayers. Let's take for instance if you come from a family that is under a curse of poverty. This means people don't get rich in that kind of family. In such cases people in the family would always be having dreams of being in poverty because of the foundational curse in the family. A curse is a curse, but a curse without a curse shall not stand (Proverbs 26:2), and so therefore we must know how to fight these spiritual powers in order to destroy them completely and prevent such problems in the family. Adequate fasting, prayers, holiness and righteousness must be a lifestyle if we want to get out of a curse quickly and permanently. When there are evil curses or covenants in a family then your dream life would always be manipulated. Great deliverance through prayer and fasting would be needed to change this kind of situation. The way we handle it is what will bring about our victory over such problems. When there is an evil pattern of things happening in a family, in order for it to repeat itself there must be dark forces that help to bring them to pass through our dreams. There must also be a bridge that connects the past to the present which is sin. It does not affect those who give themselves to God and become very prayerful. Because the prayerful ones would be able to escape this kind of situation through prayers.

When you are far from God and His Commandments, it would be difficult to get out of foundational problems permanently because there will be a bridge that still connects the problem to you through sins. These are the kind of people that would ask themselves, 'why me?' or 'why my family?' without considering that they might be adding to the problem because they are far from God. Most of the time, even when we know that there's a pattern and there's a problem in the family and we pray about it and it leaves, there are moments you go back to your old ways of living and start offending God again, and the problems reoccurs. So, for victory over bad dreams and foundational battles we need a deep and growing relationship with God. Our relationship with God must not be based on what you want because we cannot pretend to Him. We need to be submissive to His will and doctrines. We need to put Him first place and prioritize Him as the most important one in our lives. We must make up our minds to be in His will always. We must live a life that is conscious of His will. We can't have a relationship with our spouse and you keep doing what he or she doesn't like on a daily basis. No, we can't because that relationship will crash. So what about the King of Kings and the Lord of Lords, who deserves more than everything from us. He wants us to put Him as number one in our lives and to live our lives to please Him. That's why the first commandment is the greatest and most significant. You must love the Lord your God with all your heart and with all your might.... (Mark 12:30a). Close your eyes and pray this prayer: "O Lord, have mercy on me and let the Blood of Jesus purge my foundation."

What We Must Know About the Foundation and Your Dreams

It is true that through our dreams we can understand what is about to happen in our physical life when we have a discerning spirit. The beauty of our dreams as Christians is that we have been given the authority through prayers to control it, accept what is right and reject what is wrong. Dreams could also play a major role in our mood swings and behaviors, especially when the spirit of a man is being oppressed. Some dreams can become very confusing and deceiving, that is why we must pray for the spirit of discernment. Discernment is a spiritual gift that allows one to know the truth about a situation, person, place or things through the help of the Holy Spirit without being told by anyone. (See: Hebrews 5:14). Happy and blessed are those Christians who stick to the presence of the Holy Spirit every day. Joyful are those who listen to the Holy Spirit and don't grieve Him for they would be able to know deep and secret things. For some people dreams mean nothing, but the truth is, the reason that many are in problems today is because of manipulation from their dreams or meditation. For those who don't believe in dreams, they can never be in control of their lives and those are the kind of people that love to think like this: 'Whatever will be, will be,' or, 'if it's meant to happen it will happen.' This statement can destroy one's destiny because it is simply not true. This is why a lot of people in the world are not living the right life God designed for them to live and many of them are blind to the truth. Some people think because they are getting what they want it means they are blessed, but if they knew the original plan God had for them they would realize that they are actually living below standard. Some dreams come from God and some from the devil and his angels, so I am going to explain how to know the source of your dreams in relation to our foundation because some dreams can also come as revelation and still be a foundational dream. While others can come as mere things that want to manifest in our lives. When God wants to speak to us about something He uses dreams most of the time. God may want to tell us what caused a situation, what is about to happen if we don't pray, the plans He has for us or the things He needs us to change about ourselves. The only way we can interpret this is by the help of the Holy Spirit in the spirit of our minds. The devil and his agents could appear in our dreams in order to steal, kill, destroy, divert, confuse or manipulate things so that our physical lives will be troubled. Only discernment and strategic prayers can make us conquer this.

Additionally, what we think of most, what we love the most, where our heart is (Matt 6:21), what we do daily, could manifest in our dreams and this could be either positively or negatively. I pray that the power of discernment shall be given to you by God so you can begin to take over all the territories of your life if you are not doing that already.

Our minds can easily be manipulated by forces, especially forces that know us well called Familiar spirits. Familiar spirits are wrong spirits who work along with demonic forces to fulfill evil assignments on earth which include foundational issues. They usually appear in our dreams in the form of faces we are familiar with. They are great agents of manipulation and deceit. A person can easily form a covenant with them because they come in faces that we are close to in order to deceive us and achieve whatever evil they want to achieve in the life of the dreamer. They have the power to bring many problems into the life of someone through evil programming, and they also divert people's blessings by collecting it. Their dreams are very manipulative and this usually happens to people who have a bad foundation. It's only a prayerful and a discerning person that can overcome them. Most of the time many people think they are just dreaming about a close relative but the truth is, the reason they come in Familiar faces is to be deceptive so that they can achieve something in our dream life in other to manipulate people's original life. They use our family history, our personal history, what we do, what we say, what we like, what we agree with, what we love to eat and many other things about us to influence our dreams. The reason why bad things happen when they are not supposed to is only because it has already taken place in the spirit realm and was not reversed. I used to have interactions with a set of people sometime ago in my life and it was in a place I always wanted to go to. Because of my nature, I noticed that I would plan to be nice to them but I ended up not being nice or ended up looking proud. When such uncontrollable things happen it's because of spiritual manipulation. And so I ended up having a bad feeling that made me keep my face like someone who was angry throughout my stay there. And even when my heart wasn't angry, my attitude wasn't showing what my heart wanted. This is what evil programming and manipulation can do. It took discernment for me to understand that human attitudes can be controlled and manipulated too. It was not really my intention but something would just happen and things turned out badly. Most of these things are programmed to happen in our dreams through familiar spirits. Sometimes when we dream of things happening to other people, it is usually something the evil forces are trying to bring to pass in our lives.

Our dreams are really complicated. It can be confusing at times and with different meanings and this is why we need the Holy Spirit to help us figure out the intentions of our dreams. You can pray this prayer before you move on: "Any evil projection for my life through dreams, you shall not manifest. Die, in the name of Jesus." Also, you can say, "Everything that familiar spirits have stolen from my life, I recover you back." Also declare, "My life will not go according to the agenda of evil programmers, but it will go according to the agenda of the Holy Spirit in Jesus' name." It's important to be aware of the harm these dark forces can do or else one can never live their original life here on earth.

CHAPTER 4

Curses or Covenants in the Foundation

The first thing to do to get out of any foundational bondage or problem is to break the curse and covenant that exists it the family line. This is the first and most important step in changing any evil family pattern and becoming free from it. In order to deal with curses and covenants we must first be born again and living a life of righteousness and holiness. Hebrews 12:14 says that without Holiness no man can see the Lord. One very vital thing that God needs from His children is for His children to possess Holiness and righteousness (Luke1: 75). So in order to have a life free from challenge we need to obey God. Don't get me wrong, there are always troubles coming our way in our daily life but in order to be victorious we must be living our lives for God alone. The Bible says many are the afflictions of the righteous but the Lord delivers them from it all (Psalm 34:19). This means that as a child of God even in difficulties we are supposed to be living a triumphant life. Difficult times are supposed to be times we can learn to grow spiritually (read James 1:2).

Covenants are conscious or unconscious agreements. They could be written or spoken covenants and could either be by us or done on our behalf. It usually requires a particular conduct in order to get a certain promise from either God, man or maybe the devil. Curses are usually punishments given whenever the covenants are broken. The Bible says a lot about covenants and from reading it we can understand that our God is a covenant keeping God. He keeps His covenant with those who are faithful and obedient to His dictates (read Psalm 105: 8-11; Exodus 2:24). Also, the blood of Jesus is our everlasting covenant that has been shed for many for the forgiveness of sin (Matt 26:28). Curses started from the time of Adam and Eve, when Adam was given an instruction in the Garden of Eden not to eat the forbidden fruit and then he was convinced by Eve to do so (read Genesis 2 and 3 for better understanding). This clearly shows that the consequences of breaking laws are curses. So when covenants are kept they bring us safety, and when they are broken they bring curses and negatively affect people. The only one true covenant that is worth keeping and adhering to is the one with God. Any other one that is outside the will of God is bad. Curses and covenants are the foundation and the source of many problems we are facing today. They are the source of many sicknesses, poverty, hardship, sudden death, and oppression upon the lives of men today.

Remember that this doesn't depend on just an individual's sin, it also could be because of the sin of their ancestors or parents.

A covenant could be good or bad. The powerful thing about covenant is that once it is established it usually is attached to strong forces that back it up and make sure it is kept functioning and achieving its aim in the lives of the individuals involved. Some covenants could be harder to break, especially a blood covenant. This is because there is life in the blood and so whenever life is involved in a covenant it's always powerful. This is why the precious blood of Jesus has great significance in our lives and cleanses our sins. When we are in the right covenant even in trials and temptations there would be joy, peace and victory for us. Those who have a good foundation have a solid and unshaken covenant with God. They are confident of this because they keep their ways right with the Lord. They cannot dwell on the devil's schemes and suggestions because they know they lived their lives to please God and so they have inner peace about their future. The beauty of having a covenant with God is that you can feel it working for you in both your spiritual and physical realm. It makes you who you are because the most important thing in life is to have God as your Master and Savior and anyone who doesn't have this covenant is not a child of God. Once our covenant is established with God, we must work daily and ensure we do not break the covenant so that the consequences of breaking covenants, which are curses, do not manifest in our lives. Knowing that our work with God is not perfect and we must grow in Christ daily we must be quick to repent of our unconscious or unintentional sins. Never forget that I have told you that it's sin that brings curses, especially from an unrepentant heart. Those with a good foundation maintain their covenant work with God daily.

For those that make a covenant with the devil it always ends up with terrible consequences. The thing about this type of covenant is that it could be conscious or unconscious. Meaning many are in covenant with the devil and don't even know it. Some may even think they have covenant with God but it's not working for them because they are not careful to keep the rules of the covenant and they love to practice willful sin. Having a covenant with the devil makes one an agent of destruction and this could be knowingly or unknowingly. When you look at the behaviors of some Christians that claim to be born again you would be wondering why they are partaking in evil deeds and still call themselves Christians. Well, most of the time such people are already initiated unconsciously into the devil's covenant but feel they are Christians because they go to church. Have you ever heard the saying that, 'Who you obey is your master.' Anyone that partakes in the doctrines of the devil and his agents are not true followers of God. For some that have willfully dedicated their lives to the devil consciously, they usually have evil powers that they can use against people to manipulate and fulfill the purposes of Satan on earth. This set of people are merciless and cruel and they meet their downfall anytime they want to attack a true child of God.

Some people also make covenant with men which usually has a bad effect on them later. This could be by blood or by swearing an oath. Some even use diabolical means to make such covenants. Those who do this have just succeeded in recreating their own destiny. Apart from the usual marital vows which are scriptural, any other vow to keep a promise with someone has a backfiring effect. The fact that no one knows tomorrow and no one can predict what will happen next is why we cannot just make oaths carelessly. Some people make oaths for love, money, power, etc. Some even delve into occultism or witchcraft and make life threatening oaths. And when something later changes and the oath can no longer be fulfilled they begin to face the consequences and disaster they paid for.

Additionally, curses could be from God. The first people to bring curses to man like I mentioned before were Adam and Eve by eating the forbidden fruit. There are many scriptures in the Bible which talk about how God cursed people who refused to repent from their ways. We can also find scriptures that show the blessing for obedience and the curse for disobedience. A good one to read often is Deuteronomy 28 which is popular for Bible scholars. So the only way to escape curses is total obedience, repentance and forsaking of sins. Most of the people that have family pattern problems are under curses from God because of ancestral sins or personal sin. It is written that a curse without a curse cannot hold (Prov 26:2), therefore total obedience leads to total freedom from curses. To overcome a repeated flow of affliction in a family, a curse must be broken. Remember that a curse would have never been there if a sin did not take place. Truth is, no one can labor under a cause that God did not allow. So if anyone needs to make their way right with God and start to receive His deliverance, this is the time to say this prayer: "My Father, any sin committed by me, my parents, or my ancestors that is making me labor under a curse, I ask for mercy and let the blood of Jesus, cancel them today in Jesus' name." You can use Galatians 3:13-14 as a reference for this prayer.

Curses from the devil have to do with breaking his rules. For instance, if a man or any member of his family line made a covenant with the devil and they try to break free from it. It's a tough battle, especially if it has to do with idol worshipping in the family; also, if it has been going on in the family for decades. Such things are backed up by demonic forces and it would take a Christian who is godly and fervent in prayer to win such battles. These powers don't give up easily, especially when there is an evil dedication in the family. If you belong to a family that still practices idolatry, it's not a small problem so you have to be very serious with your salvation. The Bible says many things about the punishment for those who worship another god, in fact, most of the people who got punished in the Bible were punished either for idolatry or for disobedience. So for anyone who has a family evil covenant still existing in their family it's time to buckle up and become very close to God. The mercy of God is ultimate for a foundation built on idolatry, only the mercy of God can help people get out of the punishment they suffer for another person's sins.

Another type of curse is a curse from men. Unfortunately, curses from men are very common because we live in a world where people use their words carelessly when angry. The mere fact that a curse is a word said when angry is why the Bible talks about bridling our tongue and keeping it from speaking evil (Proverbs 21:23; 1 Peter 3:10). In a world where people argue every day and there is so much lack of wisdom in settling disputes, curses are a regular occurrence because a lot of people just don't get it that there is power in the tongue. The Bible states that the tongue has the power of life and death (Proverbs 18:21). Some people grew up saying cursing words every day, and so they count it as nothing. Being ignorant of how powerful the tongue is, some have unconsciously and unknowingly cursed others for life. There are some mothers who have a bad temperament and they use curse words on their kids when they get upset. A mother should always say a blessing to her child, even when angry. This will help to prevent future problems for her child. A curse could also be said because of a wicked act that has taken place like rape, killing, false accusations or some other bad situations. We may never know or remember when we were cursed and why we might be going through certain challenges we may be facing because of carelessness. Some people with a wicked heart may even go out of their way and say a curse against another person on an evil altar in a diabolic way. These things can be a source of long-term problems. But It can only be known and dealt with by revelation and by the grace of God.

Breaking Curses and Covenants

Awareness: To break a Curse or a Covenant we must first be aware that it exists. Some people are ignorant of its existence and they believe that things just happen because they are meant to happen. The awareness comes from looking at the lives of other people outside your family and finding out what blessings they enjoy from God that isn't working in your family. These things include whatever is normal to have as a child of God, e.g., riches, children, success, peace and many others. The Bible says there is no good thing the Lord withholds from them that work rightly according to His purpose (Psalm 84:11). It also says that the blessing of God makes a man rich and adds no sorrow (Proverbs 10:22). It also says all things work together for good for them that love God and are called according to His purpose (Romans 8:28). So if your life is not going according the standard of God's word, then you know that something is wrong. It's either you are fighting ancestral battles or you are breaking God's covenant attached to His word which makes one be under a curse. So, being aware that there is a problem is the first step to fixing the problem.

Understanding Dreams: The state of your dreams is the state of your life. The ability to dream and remember and also discern it appropriately is one key for victory in the battle of foundational curses and covenants. With the help of the Holy Spirit we all have the grace to interpret dreams. It depends on your spirituality. If one is unable to interpret their dreams, they should get help from someone who is capable of doing it. Understanding your dreams helps to channel your prayers the right way. If one is praying the wrong prayer the problem will never go away. The truth is just one prayer point can solve 1,000 problems, but we need discernment through the help of the Holy Spirit, our teacher (John 14:26). If we do not connect to Him we would be in so much confusion about our spiritual lives. And if we do not know the right words to say, the problems will remain.

Know the Source: After we have discerned a dream or we have been able to understand the pattern of problems in our family, the next thing to do is to know the root of the problem and then you can attack it from the root. Not knowing the root of your problem will only lead to prolonged battles and wrong prayers. Anything that is destroyed from the root doesn't have power to stand strong again. The root of your battles can be revealed to you by revelation too, if you pray the right prayers. You can pray this type of prayer, "Oh, Lord! Show me the source of my problems in Jesus' name." Or you can say, "Any power behind my problems be exposed by fire in Jesus' name." These are just some of the examples of prayers that can be used for inquiry or to know the source of a problem.

Restitution: Restitution simply means restoration of something back to normal. If there is a problem that can be solved by physical confrontation and addressing the issues, do not hesitate because many are in bondage because they failed to restitute. For instance, if you offended someone and the person laid a curse on you out of grief and you know that person is still alive, then the right thing to do is to go and make peace. It is important for that offended person to acknowledge that they have forgiven you or at least hear you say that you are sorry. Restitution sometimes brings deliverance instantly. This may not be true in all cases, but for the ones that could be solved that way please do so immediately. Sometimes forgiveness brings fast breakthroughs because we can never know the lengths some people can go to repay evil for evil and also we cannot predict the relationship the person you offended has with God. We must always try to be at peace with all men. If not, our prayers might not be accepted (read Matt 5:23-24).

Strategic Prayer: This has to do with praying deliberately to solve a particular issue. So, our foundation needs total restoration but we must be strategic because marathon prayer consumes time. With my experience in prayers I have noticed that some prayers take a longer time to be answered than others and in such cases we must be able to pray appropriately. Some people can use one prayer point, some can use ten and some can use forty prayer points before they see any results. Prayers will be more effective when they are specific. There are some prayer points that can solve many other problems. Let's look at the life of Solomon who asked God for wisdom and then God gave him great wisdom that was attached to wealth, influence and fame. We must learn to pray strategic prayers so we do not get confused and worn out. The Holy Spirit still remains the best helper with these types of prayers.

Repentance: This is a very important step to break free from foundational curses and covenants. We cannot say we want to be free from something and we are busy doing what caused it in the first place. For those who have ancestral or parental sins, evil curses or covenants, we cannot be praying to God for help and still be working in the old ways of our parent or forefathers. For Christians, repentance means changing our ways and following the ways of righteousness and Holiness. We must get rid of the old man and put on the new man. Any Christian that wants a permanent solution to their problem must be ready to do the right things by living in holiness and righteousness. We must not be deceived that only our prayers would save us. God cannot be mocked, whatever a man sows that will he reap (Galatians 6:7).

Consistency: Life is a battle and only the righteous will end in victory. There is no battle free life, but there are people that live their lives above battles and this is the power of laying a good foundation. To be consistent in this scenario means maintaining your deliverance and keeping our covenant with God. To keep our battles from reoccurring we must be known as "Fire Christians." Fire Christians means being known for your seriousness with the things of God. The Bible says that if an unclean sprit leaves a man it will come back to check if his house (which is his body) is kept clean or not, and if not he goes and brings seven more wicked spirits to stay with him in the same place he left before (Matt12: 43-45). So we must be actively praying and reading the word of God always so we do not make room for reoccurrences of old problems in our lives. The Bible says put on the new man (Ephesians 4:24). If we call ourselves Christians we must never go back to our old way of living. God will not give to us what we cannot keep. We must maintain our deliverance.

CHAPTER 5

How to Live Victorious in Christ and Repair Our Foundation

So far so good, we have understood from this book that our foundation is the key to success or failure in life. The word of God says it does not depend on human desire or effort but on God's mercy (Romans 9:16). This means that for whom the Lord shows mercy, success is guaranteed. The conclusion of the matter is that the one and only way out of foundational battles is to embrace God completely and be His friend. There's no other way to overcome this. If we try to use human effort and wisdom it won't work because we are very carnal in nature, and without God we cannot fight and win any battle because we do not war after the flesh (Ephesians 6:2). We must embrace the fact that we are spirit beings having an experience as a human being. We must embrace our spirituality and then start to live our lives above the physical by sowing into spiritual things regularly. You can read Romans 8:6-10 for more understanding. This chapter will explain to you in various ways how we can get closer to God, how we can sow to the spirit and starve the flesh and how we can win battles as Christians. But first of all, bear in mind that when someone decides to change their ways and turn to God genuinely, it frustrates the kingdom of darkness. This is different from proclaiming that you are a Christian or even working in the church. It has to do with making God the number one decision of your life. It's not just a dedication of life but a dedication of self. It's about putting on the new man and forsaking the desires of this world. It's about not compromising your faith and loving God deeply. It's about hating anything that makes God angry with you. It's about being spiritually minded and not carnally minded by not caring about the pleasures and goals of this world. But solely caring about fulfilling God's purpose for us and making Heaven. It's about saying to ourselves, this is not our last bus stop and we must be among those in heaven when the roll is called up yonder. Having this mindset is the only way we can overcome and live above the world's battles. So, here is how can we achieve this:

Get Closer to God: Getting close to God is not as many people in the world see it. I know a lot of people who think they are close to God just because their prayers are answered but truth is they are not on the same boat with God. God can decide to answer anyone's prayers but God has His inner circle which can also be known as His disciples just like any other person on earth has a closer companion. Knowing God is ultimate in order to become one of His disciples. A lot of people think they know God but knowing God is much deeper than just reading the Bible or going to church or evangelizing from His Kingdom. God desires for us all to be closer to Him but He has given us free will. He doesn't need us at all, we are the ones who need Him and we need to embrace His love. So in getting closer to God we must first be sanctified. We must be cleansed inside out and be freed from negative and ungodly thoughts and attitudes. We must be a good landing space for the Holy Spirit. We must be accessible by the Holy Spirt because He is a teacher and can make us know God more. Another way of knowing God is by listening to preachers who have been serving Him for a long time. This set of people would have been used to God's ways and have enough knowledge about Him by experience. Some people get to know God by praying about it. God searches the heart of man and can reveal Himself to anyone whose heart is fit for it.

Also, the Bible says that my sheep know my voice (John 10:27-28), this means we must follow God as He is our shepherd and we are His sheep. So therefore we must be led by Him at all times. Our everyday activities must be committed into His hands, we must be ready to follow His guiding without being rebellious or reluctant. We must be humble enough to forget our own wants and needs and embrace what He wants us to have. We must not argue with what He wants us to do. We must take discipline and any form of hardship as part of our process for becoming spiritually grounded. We must seek to please Him at all times with our actions. We must not be people pleasers but God pleasers. For instance, if God tells us to give up something we love the most to follow Him, we must be willing and ready because that is only what will make us be His disciplines and come into His inner circle. Those who belong to His inner circle fear Him. They know the importance of being in God's perfect will and having the fullness of His presence in them.

Sow to the Spirit and Starve the Flesh: To sow in the spirit is what we do to grow spiritually. We must take our spiritual life seriously and do the extra work to maintain it. By reading the Bible daily we are setting our minds on spiritual things. Bible reading should be like soul food. I honestly cannot do without reading my Bible daily. No matter how tired I am, I still try to read and get some understanding and trust me it is like healing in my soul. It completes me and makes me feel whole. I always tell people this about me and they think I am too spiritual. Well, being spiritual for things of God is definitely a goal for me.

Another thing is to be careful not to sin, by not committing willful sin we get a better chance of overcoming our battles without the enemy confronting us because our sins give the enemy a foothold. I battled with my sins when I was trying to improve my spiritual life. But when God is really interested in using you He begins to train and chasten you to fit into what He wants. What I am trying to say here is with God nothing is impossible. If we think we are too bad and we cannot change, then try God by praying the right prayers and see what He would do. Some of the prayers we can use for this case are, "Father, have mercy on me and give me the grace to do Your will," or say, "Lord, anything that I am doing that will make me miss heaven, give me grace to overcome." You can also say, "Father, please give me no other option than to do Your will." Trust me, these kinds of prayers move heaven and when you begin to see yourself changing your ways it's going be like a dream to you. God will give you the adequate wisdom and strength to overcome your sins.

Another way to sow to the spirit is to avoid fights, arguments, or retaliation. The main reason we do all these things is pride and self-love. We must become a fool in the physical to become powerful in the spirit. The Bible says turn the other cheek when we are being attacked (Matt 5:39). The feeling that we are too important to be humiliated is just pure pride. Was our Father, Jesus Christ not humiliated? We need to calm down and live our lives as Children with identical characters with their Father, Jesus Christ. We must endure what our Heavenly Father endured, we must accept what our Heavenly Father accepted, we must behave how our Heavenly Father behaved with people. We must be free from unforgiveness and bitterness and hatred because these are the real killers of anointing. If we hate our earthly brother we see, then how can we now love our Heavenly Father we do not see (1John 4:20). If we don't show others who offend us mercy, we should not expect to be shown mercy too. A true child of God must be full of love and mercy and not regard the flaws and wrongdoings of others as much.

Another way of sowing to the spirit is to be a good financial giver in the things of God. The things we spend our money on is where our heart is. Being able to invest in the things of God makes you a true candidate for uncommon blessings. True lovers of God Almighty will do anything to make the kingdom move forward which includes investing in the things of God and adding to the growth and development of their churches. Sowing to the spirit also involves helping the less privileged because the Bible says that whoever is kind to the needy, honors God (Proverbs 14: 31). Putting a smile on the faces of people who have no other alternative in life. It is also a wonderful way of getting God's attention for restoration and breakthrough in our lives.

Frequent prayer, fasting, Bible reading and evangelism should be the lifestyle of those people who want God to fight for them. We must be able to dedicate a sufficient part of our day and off work days for His activities. The more we do His work the more we know Him, the more we want to know Him the more He reveals Himself to us. The more He reveals Himself to us the more we become wise, the more wisdom we have the more victory we would get in the battle of life. Putting God first is never a waste of time, even the Bible says when we put Him first all other things would be added to us (Matt 6:33). So to gain total victory from these foundational battles we must have the things of God in our heart all the time. This is so possible, never think it isn't because what you love the most is what you think of the most. And if you think loving human beings more than God will get you what you want in life you will be so disappointed sooner or later because no human, child, husband, mother, best friend, etc., can be as loyal, loving, forgiving, and helpful as He is. We have to be a God lover and a God pleaser because He is a miracle worker and will do for you what no man can ever do.

Total Obedience: This is when we live a lifestyle of obedience to the doctrines of the Bible. It also means being careful to obey the dictates and instructions of the Holy Spirit in us. We must say no to willful sin or secret sin. Knowing the truth is not enough but practicing what we preach is key. True children of God get instruction from the Holy Spirit either during their quiet times or even when they are in a busy place. The ability to listen to and obey the Holy Spirit without hesitating or postponing the obedience makes us qualified for more anointing from God and anyone with anointing will continue to win spiritual battles. God gives His power and anointing to those who are deeply obedient and purified. It also means not giving room for compromising or peer pressure in the things of God. It means total discipline in doing the things of God and not adhering to what we feel about it but focusing on what pleases God.

Fulfill Your Destiny

This is actually the most important thing in our lives on earth. And yes, it is more important than having family, money, power, or fame. Everyone has a destiny and as

I mentioned earlier and in order for us to be free from battles we must seek to become who God wants us to be and also do what God created us to do. Everyone on earth has a divine agenda but some are totally in the wrong part because they are not aware or ignorant. Some people have been diverted and are not doing or being what God has created them to be. It takes prayer to know God's agenda for our life. Some people know their divine agenda from dreams, visions, inspiration or maybe a prophet. In my case I had a very hard foundation that almost took my life and the only way I could find out was after going through deep deliverance. Beloved, I was in bondage but God got me out and called me His own and He can do the same for you too.

So it works differently for us all. If we are fulfilling our destiny, God will automatically fight our battles and give us victory. Another thing we must all know is that no one has a destiny that does not have to do with glorifying God. If we think we are doing what He asked us to do but we are not glorifying Him with our works then we will fall back into a bad foundation and the devil will take over. The choice is ours, choose your lifestyle wisely and be among those who came to this battleground we call the world and saw many difficulties, yet conquered them all. We can never do it on our own. It's not by power or by might, but by the Spirit of God (Zechariah 4:6).

Printed in the United States
by Baker & Taylor Publisher Services